*This guide can open the door, but it will be up to you to follow the path………*

When you hear people talking about the amazing beaches they saw online or the awesome trip their best-friend just came back from it is only natural to want to take part in similar adventures. So, why aren't you? There are probably numerous answers to that question, just a few might be:

I can't afford it.

I don't know how to start.

Where do they get the deals?

How do they afford it?

The only question I cannot answer for you is…. **WHY**? Why do you want to travel? Traveling the world will change the very person you are at this moment. Good experiences, awkward situations, adventures, roadblocks, stress, and so much more will shape the new you. Keep in mind throughout this guide that nothing written within this guide is meant to hurt your feelings or make you feel dumb. In essence, it's meant to do the exact opposite and hopefully open your eyes to the many possibilities that are right in front of you. You have made the biggest decision already and that is to begin. I want to give you that final push and show you that traveling the world is a possibility and can be done efficiently and effectively.

Every single tip in my book has come from personal experience while traveling through 100 plus countries across 6 continents and stepping foot on all 50 states over the last 36 months. Some of these tips were discovered through very hard lessons being learned. Traveling the world can be scary and there should always be a slight bit of fear in someone who is traveling to new and uncharted lands. There is absolutely nothing wrong with the fear of the unknown, but that is also what gives you that feeling. That feeling that none of us can describe. That feeling that has us up the night before a flight even though we know we should be sleeping. Excitement, motivation, fear, and desire are all emotions that many people experience before traveling. Traveling is a skill like any other and it needs to be practiced for you to become better. If you can learn from others' mistakes and continue to push forward, then you can and will become a more effective traveler. I hope the following 101 tips & tricks can help push you in the right direction and help you begin that journey you have always wanted to start.

**Contact Information**

- *Instagram@biggersworld*

- *Facebook@biggersworld*

- *Youtube@biggersworld*

- *TiredOfWorking.com*

- *BiggersWorld Amazon Store*

# Your Journey Starts Now.....

1.  **Do some research!!** It will pay off!! Research is crucial when planning a trip. I know you have probably heard the saying, *"just go with the flow,"* a million times but this isn't practical for 99% of people planning trips because they have time restraints. Therefore, do a few hours of research and this can lead to alleviating tons of heartache and headaches.

2.  **Try local foods but be cautious**. Local food is amazing and is the highlight of many travelers' trips, but it is necessary to always be prepared for the worst. Food poisoning happens all the time throughout the world, so you need to be ready. Carry a travel-sized *Pepto-Bismol* and your trip could be saved.

3.  **Travel Insurance is a must**. I didn't think this was true until my most recent trip to Bali, Indonesia in 2018. After a brief conversation with my tour guide, I was convinced, rather easy if I may add, that jumping off a 40-foot cliff into murky water was a good idea. I was assured by my tour guide that

it would be deep enough, but I soon found out that was not completely accurate. Jumping off a 40-foot cliff into 3 feet of water doesn't do very well for the ankles. My ankle quickly swelled up and I was on crutches for the next 10 weeks. Use this example as an incident to learn from. This was a dumb decision on my part which lead to several additional travel inconveniences. You may be reading this saying, *I'd never do that*, but you don't know what you'll do until the situation is upon you. Travel insurance is not expensive and well worth it. Worldnomads.com is a great website to start with. Also, several credit cards offer free travel insurance so look give your credit card company a call.

4. **Have extra passport photos.** These photos can be picked up nearly anywhere camera film is developed. Many airports will have a passport photo printout stand available where you can get several photos simultaneously. When you are getting your visa, you may need an additional photo. Having multiple passport photos on hand can help you avoid ridiculously long lines at the airport arrival counter.

5. **Daypacks should have your valuables in them.** Airbnbs, hostels, and hotel rooms are all vulnerable to theft. I'm not saying pack every single valuable item in your day bag every day but it is smart to bring the absolute essentials. Passports, cellphones, and a credit card should always be in your day bag.

6. **Remember that the people in your destination do not know who you are, you can be who you want to be (be careful not to get carried away).** This is regarding newbie single travelers for the most part but could be used by anyone. When traveling alone, it is easy to become intimidated by new people and new surroundings. However, remember that nobody there knows who you are. You can be anyone you want to be. I'm certainly not saying to lie to people because that is wrong, but that does not mean you have to be the same person you are back home. If you want to be the athletic guy or gal who gets up and runs in the morning and comes back sweaty when everyone else is eating their free breakfast at the hostel, then do it. This is the time to be who you want.

7. **Take photos with you in them.** Take photos with you in them, not just your surroundings. I've come across many travelers who tell me about all these great experiences but then realize they took no pictures of their adventures with themselves in them. Don't be afraid to ask someone nearby to take your picture. People are much nicer than you may anticipate. Another suggestion would be to bring a tripod. Amazon sells them for 10$ and they are collapsible and take up minimal room.

8. **A few words go a long way.** Learning just a few words of the local language of the country you are visiting can alter the local people's perception of you by a million percent. Many foreign people I have come across love to practice English but may be nervous to begin the conversation. So, if you try to say a few words in their language and sound a little ridiculous, then it will allow them to open themselves up much easier. I've seen this work firsthand and it goes double for Paris, France. I mean this in no bad way, but visiting Paris can be tricky when interacting with locals. However, during my most recent trip, I tried to speak

French and the locals loved it. The locals had no issue in speaking English with me after they say me try French. I have travel colleagues that choose not to do what I'm suggesting, and they had much worse experiences. *"A few words go a long way."*

9. **Earplugs are a must.** Earplugs may be the most important item to bring on a trip. If you are a light sleeper like me, then they are 100% the most important item. A human body cannot function without sleep. That's not fake news, that's a fact. Spend a few bucks and always have earplugs.

10. **A space-saver bag can make all the difference.** Space-saver bags can be purchased at amazon.com and will allow you to take all the clothing you want and instantly reduce the amount of space it occupies by at least half. They are a worthy investment and one bag can last months before it needs to be swapped out.

11. **Be observant while taking photos, not everyone wants to be in your photo.** Sometimes we want to take a picture so fast due to our excitement. This is a great feeling to have but remember to be courteous to those around you. The

people around you may not want to be on your Instagram feed and may even be offended by you taking the picture with them in the background. Example: At a Columbian soccer match I watched a tourist get his smartphone smashed on the ground by a local because he took a picture during the match and the guy was in the background. Some people don't want to be in your pictures!

12. **Planning can allow you to see more, but you'll never have time to see it all.** This is a golden rule for me. The first topic I spoke about was researching because it can allow you to see more in the time you have. Keep in mind that when you are limited on time, you won't be able to see everything you want but that is okay. Prioritize what you want to see and just check as many things off the list as you can in the time you have. Monitoring the weather can also improve your chances of seeing more.

13. **Remember to take a moment a day and just smile.** You are traveling the world and many people would love to swap places. Smiling for 30 seconds at breakfast is something I like to do each morning. It's somewhat humorous because

I've been at breakfast and had people giving me the weirdest looks. I had no idea why until I realized I had been smiling and starring into space for the last few minutes.

14. **Jet lag is real and you will be tired, so plan for it.** Jet lag affects everyone differently but if you are taking a 15-hour flight and think you are going to get off the plane and crush the day, you may want to re-think this idea. Jet lag will catch up to you, so try to plan for it. If you can, try and allow yourself a day to get back in the right headspace. This can be done by simply making your first day in the country a free day. If you are up for exploring, then go get it on. If not, then take it easy and go hard the following day and wake up bright and early. Sunrise and the 3 hours following are prime time to see a city before everyone else wakes up.

15. **Keep track of your money.** It will go faster than you think. In personal experiences, my paper money is spent so much faster than I plan for. Also, the cash conversions are often hard to remember. Before you know it, the $200 you converted this morning is now down to 20$ bucks. Try to keep track of your expenses. Sit down each night and go

over what you bought throughout the day. This can help you not spend money on unneeded expenses.

16. **I pack one week out before I start a trip**. It may seem pointless, but I assure you it is not. It's a great habit to develop and often I remember items that need to be packed as my departure date nears. Try it once and I bet it will become a habit after you remember that charger for your electric toothbrush that you almost forgot. Don't put it off and keep telling yourself you are going to do it; you know who you are and if you are a born procrastinator!

17. **Discounts are everywhere so try to find them.** There are sites everywhere offering discounts but if you put forth no effort you are not going to find them. A great place to start is on the Google home screen and type the country you are visiting followed by the word discount. Not being lazy can save you more money than you would ever imagine, which means more fun activities that you can spend your savings on.

18. **Sunscreen is needed, but you might not know it.** This is something I see travelers make a mistake with all the time. I

know you have seen the people I'm referring to. The people that have legs that look like they belong on a lobster. Just put on sunscreen when it's sunny especially when you are in a new environment. The sun works differently in different places. It will hurt no one and could save you some real agony. A sunburn can ruin your entire trip.

19. **I get nervous before all my travels. Did I forget this? Did I plan on this?** Remember that this is natural. Write out your list and do your research. This is all that you can do to prepare. If you forget something, you will find a way to make it work. If you have the 10 essential items which I mention at the end of this book then you will be just fine. Don't worry, if you make it to the end of this book, you'll see the 10 items I'm referring to.

20. **Utilize Netflix, Apple Music, and any eBooks for use on airplanes, trains, buses and rainy days.** Download more than you think you will need beforehand. It's always a good plan to have more entertainment than you anticipate needing. A traveler cannot know how many extended layovers they may encounter. I have had way more than I

ever thought possible and sometimes that can mean sleeping in an airport. Having *"The Lion King"* on hand can make sleeping in the airport not seem as bad.

21. **Do a social media search.** Social media can help you find stuff you may want to try. Take an hour and search around social media groups and you'll be happy you did. Utilizing Instagram, Facebook and YouTube can help you discover some unusual sites or activities you may never have thought about.

22. **Don't be afraid to learn something new.** Do you want to know how to make pottery, salsa dance, or cook gourmet cuisine? If there's a way to learn, then learn it firsthand when you are in the country that made it famous. Nobody can teach you how to salsa dance better than someone who was born in Latin America and started dancing before they could talk.

23. **Certain internet sites do indeed track what we look at when we search the same topic over and over again.** Therefore, prices can go up if you search for it too many times. Beware of this and always open an *Incognito* window

so there is no search history present on that browser. If you have no idea what I'm talking about then go ahead and type *incognito browser* in the Google search engine and follow the steps.

24. **Contraception is a necessity.** Many countries do not sell the same types of sexual protection i.e. condoms like the United States. It is always better to have contraception that you trust rather than not.

25. **Take care of laptops, phones, iPads, and other electronics.** Investing in a drop-proof case can help you not have a mid-trip crisis when someone bumps you in the airport and it falls out of your hand and busts all over the ground. Be prepared and you won't have to spend an obscured amount of money to replace your electronics abroad.

26. **Charging ports are not everywhere.** In the USA, there are outlets everywhere and anywhere to charge up our devices in virtually every store. They are scattered throughout airports, restaurants, and just about anywhere else you can think of. However, this does not exist elsewhere.

Throughout Europe & Asia, I found myself wandering airports for hours looking for usable outlets and yes I had the proper outlet converter. So, what's the solution? Ensure that your phone is fully charged before leaving your accommodation or have a portable charger. This, like the majority of items I will suggest in this book, can be found on the amazon marketplace for less than $10.

27. **Bring extra battery packs.** This seems self-explanatory, but time and time again I come across travelers that have one battery for their electronics and no alkaline batteries for various other electronics. Carrying a 4 pack of AA and or AAA batteries can save the day or make you a hero among the friends you meet along your journey.

28. **Know your passport information inside and out.** Also, take a picture of your passport with your cell phone just in case you misplace it. Yes, it does happen, so don't let it be you. Another important tip is to check your expiration date before you leave. Just because your passport doesn't expire until you are getting back doesn't mean *VISA*

applications will accept your passport if you don't have at least 6 months left on the passport.

29. **Be mindful when packing clothes**. Stick with dark colors: blacks, greens, and blues can mix and match easily allowing for more outfit options. Maximize your options by having colors that all mesh together.

30. **Clothing material is huge for numerous reasons.** The first reason would be that certain material can be folded down more effectively. The less space an article of clothing takes up means the more clothing you can pack. Next, due to the various temperatures and climate you might be in, pack accordingly. If you are in cold weather, maybe you need wool or thick polyester to keep you warm. Also, if you are bringing a jacket always wear it in the airport and never pack it away taking up vital space in your baggage.

31. **Be watchful and trusting.** They sound counterintuitive. However, it can be seen daily while traveling that most of the people you meet are good people and will help you without seeking reimbursement. Even so, never be too trusting and keep your eyes open in your surroundings. In

most situations, nothing is free so be careful accepting gifts, especially in touristy locations. This also goes for advice on finding your accommodation. I have seen people expect compensation for giving you directions so be aware.

32. **Credit cards and debit cards are a must.** Make sure you check foreign transaction fees on your cards before departing. Have a few different cards just in case. Some credit cards will not charge transaction fees, and some may even allow for free travel insurance and/or discounted car rentals. Nonetheless, at nighttime only take one card out with you. Pickpocketing does happen and has happened to me. It doesn't matter how big your muscles are or how great your beard is, everyone can be a target.

33. **Emergency cash is always a good idea.** Have a hidden place in your bag where you stash some cash. I'm not saying put two hundred dollars in your sock. I'm referring to placing $20-$30 in a toiletry bag with your toothpaste just in case you need it. Being prepared can never be stressed enough while traveling.

34. **Some places won't have much research available.** Don't give up after an hour of research when nothing had been uncovered. There is always a website, magazine article, podcast or blog that will have information. Sometimes this will take you time and patience but it can be well worth the effort. Social Media has opened an entirely new door for travel.

35. **Stuff will go wrong while traveling.** This is not an if or a when but an inevitability. Injuries, food poisoning, getting scammed, and so much more can and most likely will occur if you travel enough. You must be able to roll with the punches and always remember, *you're traveling the world, so smile.* Don't lose your temper, it benefits no one. I do know this is much easier said than done, but we both know it is accurate.

36. **Take screenshots of your destinations before you get there.** I'm referring to screenshots of your map location of where you trying to go to. This will allow you to see the streets if and when your Google maps decides not to work. Also, write down the address and perhaps learn how to say,

"This is where I need to go," in the local dialect. It will go very far. I have personally seen this to be true.

37. **Jeans are important.** They always seem to take up the most room when packing in my space-saver bags. However, jeans are amazing because a good pair of Levi jeans don't need to be washed every day and can last several outings before you need to wash them again. Just make sure you are wearing them each time you travel to a new destination and they won't take up any room in your bag.

38. **Pictures and videos can be so important to someone while traveling.** So, a good plan is to upload your pictures and videos onto your social media as you go so that you will have those pictures if something happens to your camera and or smartphone. Put your profile on private and it can be used as strictly a storage backup if you choose.

39. **Should I stay away from touristy areas?** When visiting large cities, you may have been instructed to stay away from the touristy areas. This is not always a smart plan. I get it: you don't like crowds or other needy tourists. If you

plan to go at the right times, then you can avoid all of that and still see the tourist attractions. They are world-renowned famous attractions for a reason. Occasionally your mind will be blown like mine was in Kuala Lumpur, Malaysia when I went to the breathtaking *Rainbow Stairs to the Batu Caves.* Don't skip tourist attractions, just plan out how to see them without dealing with tourist chaos.

40. **Routines can be key.** I have a routine when I'm leaving an airplane where I count off the stuff that is must-have on my fingers. Passport, wallet, keys, phone, and my iPad are the 5 items I never want to leave on the airplane. I will do this after every flight while everyone else rushes to stand up before the airplane doors are even open I do my counts a few times. Your list may be different but it's a great routine to get into.

41. **Always call your banks before you plan to travel.** However, be ready for potential problems with cards even if you call your banks. That is why it is imperative to have spare cash. This has happened to me more times than I can count, and my banks continue to do it repeatedly.

Remember when you are abroad you need your bank; they don't need you so call them and be polite and make sure your cards work before you leave the airport.

42. **Proper packing is crucial.** When you're packing, only bring what you are 100% sure you need. Even after traveling half the world, I still end trips with stuff I never used. Why would I ever need three pairs of board shorts and a polo shirt to match? *I have no idea, but I have had this happen.* Go through your clothes a few times and ask yourself, *will I wear this more than once?* The answer better be yes, or it needs to stay in your closet.

43. **If you don't need souvenirs, then don't buy them.** From time to time you may feel obligated to buy some souvenirs. Don't feel like you must. Souvenirs are great but so are pictures. Once you are home, you can have the pictures made into a poster, put on a postcard, and even have the photos printed on blankets, and these souvenirs don't take up any room in your baggage.

44. **When eating, looks can often be deceiving.** If a small place has no customers, your first feeling may be that it is

no good. I have seen this to be completely inaccurate. Countries eat at different times around the world so empty doesn't necessarily equal bad. When you are hungry, perhaps the locals are not. As a rule of thumb, I go by the number of options on a menu. The fewer options there are to eat, the better the place has turned out to be. It may sound weird but give it a try.

45. **Know the travel seasons.** Each continent is different, which means there are low and high seasons in which people travel. Flights can be very cheap during these seasons. The apps *Hopper* and *Skyscanner* are amazing and they will notify you when to buy the tickets for the dates you have pre-selected.

46. **Using VPN's.** A VPN is something that has become much more useful in my recent travels. NordVPN is a simple software app that you can download that will help you use your Netflix and other programs abroad. It will put your IP address in a different country so you can stream movies, television shows, and music. This is an amazing tool because everyone can use a Netflix and chill night.

Everyone was wondering how I was watching the *Game of Thrones* finale while in Guatemala.

47. **Toiletries are packing necessities some need and some don't.** Many travelers need their hair conditioner, and some don't. There is always an argument over solids and liquids, and this will be a decision you need to make based on preference. Regardless, always remember to keep everything in Ziploc bags. The last thing you want is a leak which then spills all over the rest of your travel necessities. *Bonus tip: Pick up laundry detergent mini sheets. These can be used in place of the liquid laundry detergent and take up minimal space.*

48. **Money belts are often discussed in travel blogs.** These are a 100% personal preference. I have used them in multiple countries, but you can look a little ridiculous and nothing says "tourist" like a money belt in plain sight. However, if you feel more comfortable and at ease, don't let anyone talk you out of it. Your comfort and safety are what is most important.

49. **Travel microfiber towels are a must-bring item.**

    Microfiber towels were introduced to me in the United States Army and I've used them ever since. They take up no room and after a while, you will understand the patting motion and will be able to dry yourself in no time.

50. **Comfort Zones!** If you are traveling alone, you have already made a huge step in the right direction. Just remember that the odds of you encountering any of these people again are slim to none, so get out of your comfort zone. Be bold and go for it.

51. **Try out all your travel items before your initial departure.** I've made this mistake quite a few times. If you buy a tent that you plan to use, then try it out before you leave. Don't buy it and not try it out because it looks so pretty in its original box. Open that box and try everything out. Trial runs can make your life so much easier once you are on your trip.

52. **Currency exchanging is another area that gets a lot of debate.** Airports will often give you the worst rates. However, getting currency at the airport does ensure that

you have it. Generally, I will get a small amount at the airport and then get more cash later after I find a better rate. This is something I feel very strongly about: always have the local currency on hand because if you do not, you could find yourself in a tight spot sooner than later. Also, don't try to use American currency unless it is absolutely necessary. The local taxis will charge more or give you bogus change back as soon as they see you are paying in American currency. It's your responsibility to be prepared, not theirs. Remember that you are in their country, so be prepared.

53. **Morning flights can be good and bad, let me explain.** On the negative side, public transportation may not be running yet making it difficult to get to and from the airport cheaply. Furthermore, you may be recovering from a hangover, and/or maybe you just slept in. Be ready and packed the night prior if you find yourself in this position. On a positive note, booking morning flights can pay off in case of cancellations and you may be able to hop on a later flight to your destination on the same day in which you planned the flight.

54. **Not all countries have the internet.** When they do, it is often at a speed that could be compared to dial-up. This is something that can make some people so frustrated but remember that you are the one traveling, so be ready for this. If it happens, just embrace it and take a walk. If you can locate a Starbucks, then you may be in luck because they generally have a very good internet connection regardless of where you are located.

55. **Are my sandals my shower shoes?** A 2-in-1 combo is ideal for traveling. I have a pair of *Keens sandals* that I wear for both outdoors and in the shower. Just remember how many people use those showers at hostels and/or hotels. Often, I have seen people treat hotel bathrooms much worse than hostel bathrooms. Don't forget your shower shoes.

56. **Planning can allow for better travel deals.** I will usually start to plan my trip 4-6 months out and have the essentials booked a month prior. Also, having your first & last destination planned can go a long way. The essentials include flight, transportation, and lodging. Discounts and

special offers will be much easier to find a few months out. If you have procrastinated be sure to check out *Last Minute Deals* on *Travelzoo.com*

57. **Check your phone for SIM card capability.** Can you prepay with your phone carrier? Can you use the phone service over Wi-Fi? Have this all planned before your trip. Bad news for iPhone users. If your phone is not completely paid off you are going to have issues trying to use a sim card abroad so make sure you verify how to use wifi calling beforehand.

58. **Hostels can become redundant.** When staying in hostels for a long stay i.e. months try to schedule one night a week or every two weeks at a cheap hotel and/or Airbnb. These accommodations are often not that much more expensive, and a night away from the hustle and bustle of a hostel can go a long way.

59. **Leave all your preconceived notions and judgments at home.** This is something that can be very hard to do. The important thing is to catch yourself if you are casting judgment. People washing in the streets and or brushing

their teeth in the open is just a part of life in some countries. Let's not even talk about the bathroom situation in some locations, but it is not our job to change the ways these activities are done. Adapt and be happy that you are experiencing these cultures. Remember that this is not your home country and try to go with the flow.

60. **Cameras versus iPhone**. In recent years, this has become a big topic of interest amongst travelers. My smartphone of choice is the iPhone and I know at least a quarter of the readers are rolling their eyes, but my iPhone has served me well from the iPhone 7 to the newest iPhone 11 pro max. However, I still carry a camera as well. My camera of choice is a Sony Alpha 6000. A great camera may be able to catch moments that an iPhone cannot. So, if you can bring a nice camera, I would encourage you to take one along. Just keep in mind that you can take nearly any picture you desire with a smartphone and not look like a human bullseye with the camera and a huge lens.

61. **Yearly physicals should be a part of life.** I like to schedule my yearly checkups before I plan an extended

trip. This lets me know that I'm good to go and the adventure can begin with nothing weighing on my mind. Coming back from a long trip also marks a good time to schedule your yearly checkup. Keeping track of your yearly physicals only sets you up for further success while traveling abroad.

62. **There are two types of experienced travelers.** Type A is a traveler who likes extended periods of travel time such as a week or a month per city. Type B is someone who can get everything done they wish to do within a matter of days. I am a traveling type B and come prepared and ready to get the show on the road as soon as I can. The moment my boots are on the ground, I'm knocking stuff off my list. Regardless of which type you are, just do your necessary research and you will be good to go.

63. **You might gain or lose weight during the trip so anticipate.** Eating abroad can be something that can confuse many travelers early in their endeavors. From a personal standpoint, I generally lose weight when traveling. Others may gain weight. Much of the world has much less

added sugars and other additives in their food than the United States. It's easier to eat slightly healthier when I travel, thus leading to a couple of pounds of weight loss. Also, being encouraged to walk everywhere will lead to weight loss. Be aware of this and monitor yourself the first month you are abroad, and you can adjust accordingly. Maybe, you will just need to add one day of exercise to even it all out if you are gaining a few unwanted pounds.

64. **Getting lost can be okay.** I wouldn't make this a habit, but sometimes it is nice just to walk a couple of miles and then stop and figure out where you are at. You never know what adventures you may come across. This is safer in countries where you have good phone service, so be sure to do your due diligence before wandering off.

65. **Round trip versus One way.** This can be a traveler's choice, but my personal choice is to buy one round trip ticket, let's say, "Miami to Berlin." Then after that, plan all one-way trips between the primary roundtrip dates, some on planes, some on trains, and some on buses. By having the roundtrip home, I know that no matter what, when I'm

ready, I just need to get to Berlin, and I'll be able to get home when the time is right.

66. **Local customs.** Just a few minutes of research can allow a traveler to feel much more at ease when they get off the plane in a new location. An example of this can be seen when I was traveling to Japan and had to get used to the difference in eye contact while conducting business. Doing a little research can expand your comfort zone and it will surely make you a better traveler.

67. **Laundry can be a hassle while traveling.** Airbnb's, hostels, and hotels may not have laundry machines, but there are generally locals that will do your laundry for a small fee. The laundry will come back clean and folded and it makes your life easier while giving to the local economy. I've used these services on multiple continents and have always had good results.

68. **Reviews are not facts.** Let's be honest: when looking at reviews, it is usually the upset person who had a bad experience who leaves the salty bias review. This is certainly not always the case but, in many situations, this is

the case. Just remember this when reading reviews and try to review multiple sources before making your own decision. A good way to do this when booking a hostel is to check the reviews on both *hosteworld.com* as well as *booking.com*.

69. **A dry bag also known as a waterproof bag can be your savior.** Countries all around the world have amazing adventures that take us to the water. A dry bag can be the savior when you find yourself on a boat and the boat captain is out of ziplock bags. A medium-sized dry bag costs only a few bucks on the amazon website and will take up very minimal room in your baggage, so just pony up the dough and grab one beforehand and your smartphone may thank you.

70. **Have a multiple USB port charger.** Most of our chargeable devices now go off USB ports. Getting a 4-in-1 USB charging station will cost you a couple of bucks and allow you to charge all equipment simultaneously.

71. **Use luggage BLING.** When traveling in and out of airports and train stations, it helps for your luggage to stand apart

from the rest. I prefer my luggage to be black, but I have bright red *BiggersWorld* patches on them to stand apart. Making your luggage easily identifiable is not just for you but even more so for the guy that hasn't slept in 20 hours and is late for a meeting and sees a black bag he thinks is his.

72. **Vitamins are needed.** Every country is different, but many foreign countries that are not the United States do not have the same vitamins you may be accustomed to getting in the states. Be sure to have at least a month's supply beforehand so you will have time to find your vitamins abroad. The same rule applies to prescriptions. Additional travel tip: you don't need to have all prescriptions in their separate bottles when going through TSA security at airports. You can have all in one pill container, just make sure you have the labels in case airport TSA ask for them. I have never had an airport TSA agent ask for my vitamin or prescription labels. I always carry a month's supply of 8-10 different vitamins.

73. **Back Pockets equals a bad idea**. Use side pockets, a cross-body, or a fanny pack can be an option but don't use the back pocket because you are asking to be pickpocketed.

74. **Restaurant Chains.** These places always seem to have reliable Wi-Fi: Burger King, McDonald's, KFC and Starbucks. Remember this the next time your Wi-Fi is only on one bar and you forgot to screenshot your accommodations. Also, use the NordVPN app that I mentioned earlier to safeguard yourself from hackers on public Wi-Fi locations.

75. **Water is a necessity.** When traveling, we often exert much more energy than we think we do. For this reason, it is necessary to drink lots of water constantly. This can be difficult at first, but it is like any habit and soon enough you will be doing it without hesitation. Another option with water is to start drinking carbonated water. Carbonated water is everywhere in Europe. Carbonated water will hydrate you the same as still water. The pink cap on the water bottles is

generally a sign of still water rather than carbonated water throughout Europe.

76. **A layover can save money.** Throughout many of my travels, I have had 18 to 24-hour layovers. These have allowed me to explore a city and/or country that I couldn't have explored without the layover. Keep this in mind when booking your flights and you just may get an added adventure. *TAP Portugal* offers this type of layovers built into their everyday flights.

77. **Have a plan or don't.** As you can probably tell, I'm a traveler that loves to have a plan. However, it can be a cool idea to arrive in a new city and just go with the flow. Take a bus downtown and go from there. This is not a regular practice of my own, but I do know many travelers that live by this rule. The best way to do this is to find a bus that will take you to the cities downtown area and begin from there.

78. **Body language is so important.** Body language is our true universal language. A smile or head nod can go a long way. This was so apparent to me when I was traveling in Krong Siem Reap, Cambodia. While walking a 1/4 mile

back from lunch, I counted 19 smiles. Nineteen separate people gave me a genuine smile and that felt great. My body language was giving off happy vibes and the locals could sense that. When's the last time you got 19 smiles?

79. **Don't Forget.** Your friends and family probably love to see your photos on social media. Remember to occasionally throw out a *hello* or *miss-you* text to your loved ones. These simple text will go a long way.

80. **Go to the local markets.** Just about every Saturday and Sunday, it is possible to find a local market where you can go and grub out on some amazing local food. They have good prices and even better food. Look for banners and signs inside the grocery stores to find out where these markets will be at.

81. **Maps.me.** Everyone has a mapping preference, but maps.me is my go-to when traveling. I carry Google maps as well but there is always smart to have two mapping apps.  I can download the offline maps of the upcoming country weeks out on both apps. Through my experience, both apps have been on point mapping wise but at multiple

times both of these apps have decided not to work. Having backups is a must when traveling abroad.

82. **Invitations can be scary.** Random invites will occur more and more while you travel, especially when you are staying in hostels. Don't turn them down unless you feel uneasy. This can help the shy get out of the comfort zone and some of my most memorable moments overseas have come from random invitations.

83. **Best translator.** This is like the above mention of maps.me and goes more on personal preference but Google Translate is my go-to. It works very well and gives me enough info to figure out my next move. Several apps have offline versions to utilize if not connected to wifi. You will not always have a good wifi connection so remember to double up on translating apps.

84. **Toilet paper.** This is a necessity for everyone but even more so for the young ladies. When traveling on buses and staying in hostels, one can find themselves desperately searching for some good ole TP in a crisis. A roll in your backpack can save you or save a buddy.

85. **Hopper, Skyscanner, Expedia & Booking.com.** Check them all before purchasing. Also, check the website of the airline or hotel that they say to be using. Sometimes you can save a few extra bucks if you buy directly from the airline or hotel. Don't forget to open an *Incognito* window.

86. **Hostel World.** When booking hostels, I like to use hostelworld.com first. I have also found that if you book directly through the hostel's website, you can get better prices and free breakfasts which are always a plus for the budget traveler.

87. **Solo, Groups, Family, Friends.** Traveling alone has always been my travel choice. When I'm alone, I'm forced to make friends and engage much more. I love the rush of meeting new people from all different backgrounds. For some, traveling alone can be very daunting at first. I assure you that if you give it a try, you may find yourself hooked.

88. **The early bird gets the worm.** Getting up early can be very difficult for some, especially if you had a night out on the town, but you can see a side of the city you never thought possible. I saw this firsthand in Bangkok, Thailand

when I got up at 5:30 am to go on a tour and it was such a wonderful sight to see. No one was around but a cleanup crew on *Khao San Road* and I could take pictures with anything and everything I wanted.

89. **Know your bag weights.** There are always ways around the system if you do your homework. Now, this is not a method that will always work, but I have used it and it has been successful many times. On many flights throughout Asia and Europe, airlines will have you weigh your bags once at the gate. If you know the weight of your bags and what it is supposed to be, then you can take out a few items while waiting in the waiting area and have someone watch them for you. Then, you walk up to the desk, weigh your bag, and receive the colored band on your bag proving you have made baggage weight. Then you can go back, get your extras, and reload. This method is not 100% but it has worked for me. I found this out when I flew into Sydney International Airport, where they weigh your bag at the very beginning before you even go through security so you

couldn't come back to get items if you left them. You got me there Sydney, Australia.

90. **Don't be a metaphorical eggplant to the employees checking you in because you will see them again.** I learned this the hard way by getting into a slight altercation in France with the employee who was checking me in. Low and behold, she was also the same employee who was checking my boarding pass to board the plane and she had me weigh my bag again. On the flip side, things tend to go smoother if you're kind to the employees. For example, I had a wonderful conversation with the gentleman checking me in while visiting Melbourne, Australia. Once at the gate, everyone's baggage around me was weighed again except mine. Be nice and ask them how their day is going. You may be surprised how far being nice can get you in the transportation sector.

91. **Plan airport pickup in advance.** When traveling from country to country, it is important to know how you are getting from the airport to your accommodations. Five minutes of research is all it takes to know if there is Uber,

Lyft, taxis, or public buses. Knowing this beforehand will help you not get scammed by the many people that will try to scam you at the airport. When I say many, I mean hundreds at some airports i.e *Bali Ngurah Rai International Airport*.

92. **Travel vest & or travel jacket.** While traveling, there have been countless times I can remember where an airline has tried to charge me for baggage. I'll be honest: I push the baggage to the limit for sure. Nobody wants to pay extra money when they don't have to. This idea goes in conjunction with the idea earlier of weighing baggage. Sometimes it's not a weighing system but a fit in EasyJet and or Ryanair container system. Check out the amazon marketplace online to get an idea of what I'm talking about when I say *travel jacket or travel vest.* I have made my own a few times by just cutting and sewing pockets into jackets I already owned, so keep that in mind.

93. **SD memory cards, USB drive, and flash drives**. All these storage devices can have a huge impact on how much you will enjoy your vacation or new lifestyle if you've decided to

go full nomad. A USB drive is the one I use the most, but I don't use it how you may think. You often will not understand the language spoken where you will be traveling, so that means you won't be able to watch movies and or television unless it is in your native tongue. So, what I do is take a 64gb USB drive and I fill it up with 25+ movies so I always have them just in case. I 100% understand that many people reading this may be rolling their eyes once again and muttering, *"When I travel, I want to see everything and I ain't got no time for watching movies."* Guess what? Sometimes mother nature does not play to your schedule. Recently, I was in Antigua, Guatemala where it rained for 5 days straight without a single break and UNO cards got old real fast. So, if you are the hostel guest that has 64gb of random movies, you may have just become the hero of the hostel.

*Another side note – Having awesome Disney and/or romantic comedies make great date proposals when it's pouring rain outside.*

94. **Check airport policy on bringing food through airport security.** This tip is as old as time, but people from all over the world still do not take advantage of it. Bring food with you on to the airplane. Especially when you are traveling on the cheaper airlines throughout Europe that will charge $28 for cheese and crackers. Airport security around the world will allow food to be brought through as long as it is packaged correctly. Nonetheless, be sure to check out the rules or just call the airport/airline and ask for verification.

95. **Volunteering can lead to free accommodations and much more.** Volunteering at hostels can earn you free accommodations and more. Every country on every continent across the globe has opportunities. A simple phone call and or email can help you discover these spots. Go on to hostelworld.com to locate potential hostels that may allow it, read through the reviews, and contact them. It may take you an hour of effort which could lead to months and months of free accommodation.

96. **A scarf or sarong can be the golden accessory.** A scarf was something I only recently discovered, and it baffles me how it took me this long to figure it out. You can use it in warm weather, cold weather, rainy weather, etc. There is always a use for a scarf, and it takes up absolutely no room. Also, you can go to the *BiggersWorld* amazon shop and get one that will hide your passport and other valuables for just a couple of bucks.

97. **Personal water bottle.** A water bottle can allow you to never pay for drinks again. Water is not free around the world; however, it is free in 99% of airports around the world. So, when you fly to your next destination, take a moment and fill it up. You can start your next journey out with a free bottle of water.

98. **Find free tours.** Free tours are becoming a more common thing in countries around the world. They aren't *completely* free, but they are free. What I mean by this is that they are free tours, but you are expected to tip at the end. There is no minimum or maximum tip. Do not hesitate to go on these tours if you don't think you have enough to tip. These tour

guides are everyday working people and they will take whatever you can afford, not to mention that a little bit from a lot of people can lead to a large amount. Find these tours by asking the hostel, hotel, and or other accommodations you have booked or go to Google and simply type: *Free Tours in* __blank__. You will be surprised at what you find.

99. **Remember that if you look the part, 99% of the time no one will say anything.** This can be true for just about anywhere and everywhere. If you look like you belong in a fancy resort and walk with confidence, then everyone will think you belong. Why is this a big deal, you ask? Hotel staff are mostly locals, which means they know where to go for the free stuff and at a bare minimum, the cheap stuff. Hotel staff has enough to deal with than to wonder if you are staying there. Just remember to look the part and they will most likely let you in and help you out without hesitation. This can also be useful to take free outside showers, pools, jacuzzies, and I've even used it to get free food at a large banquet party.

100. **Shoes, shoes, shoes.** This can be a very good investment. You need good shoes and you will most likely be walking more than you ever have before, especially if you are an American. So, prepare and spend money on good shoes and good insoles. You will be happy you did.

101. **Final Tip - Negotiation is key**. I left this tip as the final one for a reason. Haggling is an art form. It can take years of practice to become an expert, but all you need to be is good and it only takes a few words most of the time. Below I have laid out an example that I have personally used dozens of times.

Hello, are you interested,
Yes, I like that,
That is 40$
Wow, that's way more than I have,
What do you have?
I have 10$ to spend
Well for you I can do 20$
I only have 10$
Let's meet at 15$

This is only an example, but I think you get the point. If you stay strong and don't budge, generally you can get the price you feel is fair. The reason I stopped at 15$ was more for personal preference. In all reality, you could probably hold strong and get it for 10$ most of the time. However, I understand that the locals are hustling for a living. Now, as annoying as it can be for them to constantly try to haggle us, I can also respect the hustle. It's their way of making an income and we are the visitors to their country. So, out of respect for the hustle, I will more than likely compromise a small amount.

*"Remember, having sunglasses and a pair of headphones can eliminate virtually 99% of hustling interactions if that is what you prefer."*

Every situation and every single tip I have outlined in this book has been personally experienced and or utilized by myself or someone I was traveling with. In the end, none of the 101 tips I've outlined will do you any good if you don't get off your butt and make it happen. One hundred percent of people can say they are going to travel the world, but very few ever will. Even more say, "I don't know where to start, or how do you afford it?" Those questions have now been answered. All that is left to be done is for you to begin.

# BONUS for FINISHING the BOOK

## Top 10 List: "Don't leave home without!!!!!"

1. Earplugs / Sleep mask

2. Passport

3. Credit card (MasterCard or Visa because Discover and American Express are not accepted everywhere)

4. Spare cash of at least 20-30 dollars that may be needed when you are entering the new country

5. Travel size Imodium or Pepto-Bismol

6. Hand sanitizer

7. Water bottle (there are so many various kinds, just do a little research and you will find one for you)

8. Mini flashlight (just connect to your backpack, you'll be happy you did)

9. Small day bag (just shove it in your carryon bag)

10. Pen (yes, it is simple, but if you have one, then you won't have to wait in line to fill out customs and or visa forms)

# ENJOY

# YOUR

# TRAVELS

Printed in Great Britain
by Amazon

50519961R00031